CASTLES
IN THE AIR

Celia Warren
Illustrated by Karel Hayes
and Martin Melogno

A Harcourt Achieve Imprint

www.Rigby.com
1-800-531-5015

Literacy by Design Leveled Readers: *Castles in the Air*

ISBN-13: 978-1-4189-3909-0
ISBN-10:   1-4189-3909-9

Illustration Credits: Karel Hayes cover & p. 4, 5, 6, 7, 8, 9, 10, 19, 21, 23, 24, 25, 33, 34, 35, 36, 37, 39; Martin Melogno p. 11, 13, 14, 15, 17, 26, 27, 28, 29, 31

Rigby is a trademark of Harcourt Achieve Inc.

Printed in China
1A 2 3 4 5 6 7 8 985 13 12 11 10 09 08 07

CONTENTS

THE MILKMAID AND HER PAIL............5
Aesop's fable

THE BOY AND THE FOX........................11
A tale from Sweden

THE POOR MAN AND
THE FLASK OF OIL 19
A tale from India

THE THREE WISE SAYINGS....................26
A tale from Poland

THE ARCHER AND THE
RABBIT..33
A tale from Italy

THE MILKMAID AND HER PAIL

There was once a poor farmer whose daughter was always daydreaming.

"Daughter, your head is forever in the clouds," scolded the farmer. "You must come down to Earth and help me care for the animals. I need you to milk the cows."

The daughter did not care for the idea of being a simple milkmaid, but she did not want to disobey her father.

So she set off to milk the cows. But even as she collected the warm, creamy milk, her mind was far away. The daughter was lost in her dreams of far finer riches.

Before long, her work was done, and the milkmaid stepped out to the dairy, carrying her pail of fresh milk upon her head.

As she walked along, the milkmaid began to daydream about finer things and an easier life.

"The milk in this pail will provide me with cream," she daydreamed, "and the cream I shall churn into butter. Then the butter I shall take to market to sell. With the money from the sale of the butter, I shall buy a number of eggs, and these, when hatched, will produce chickens. These, in turn, will lay more eggs. Before long I shall have quite a large number of chickens. Then I shall sell some of my hens and, with the money that they will bring in, I shall buy myself a fine new gown."

The milkmaid stopped in her tracks and set down her pail of milk, swirling her imaginary skirt while she pictured the splendid gown.

"The finest silk!" she cried as she ran a finger down the length of an invisible sleeve. "And such delicate lace!" she said happily.

Next, the milkmaid raised the hem of her make-believe gown and lifted it to stroke her cheek. "The softest, thickest velvet," she murmured.

Then she sighed happily because in her mind she was now dressed like a queen!

Barely remembering that she was really the daughter of a poor farmer, she lifted the pail of milk back upon her head.

As the milkmaid continued along the path to the dairy, carrying the pail of milk like a crown, her head was in the clouds, filled with joyful, fanciful pictures.

"I shall wear my beautiful gown when I go to the fair," the milkmaid told herself, picturing herself as the center of attention. "All the young men will admire my gown and will want to talk to me and give me compliments!"

Then the milkmaid added, her nose in the air, "But I shall toss my head and turn away and have nothing to do with them."

Forgetting all about the pail, the milkmaid tossed her head as she daydreamed. Down went the pail, spilling all the milk, and all her fine castles in the air vanished in a split second!

THE BOY AND THE FOX

Long ago and far away, on the edge of a forest, there lived a farmer and her husband, along with their only child, a boy. The farmer worked hard all day in the fields, tending the crops of barley and rye. People came from far and wide to admire the fine crops in the large fields. The farmer's barley and rye sold for high prices, and slowly she and her husband grew richer and richer.

The farmer's husband worked as hard as his wife and made their home as comfortable as possible.

Every morning he baked fresh bread or a hot pie with a thick, tasty crust.

Every evening when the farmer came home from the fields, her husband had a warm fire burning in the grate, fresh flowers on the table, and clean sheets upon the beds.

As for their son, the boy wanted for nothing. His mother and father worked so hard that he had nothing to do but wander idly and think idle thoughts.

One day the boy was walking along on his way to the nearby village, lazily kicking a large stone.

At last he came to a clearing in the forest where he suddenly caught sight of a fox lying on the top of a big smooth rock.

The fox was fast asleep, so it did not know the boy had seen it.

The young boy stood quite still, watching the beautiful creature as its fur shone like bronze in the bright sunshine.

The boy loosened the belt from around his waist, slowly adjusting it to the size of a collar, and said to himself, "If I can slip this around the fox's neck, then I can capture it."

Then he added, "I shall display the fox in a special pen, and people will pay good money to come and see such a beautiful creature. With that money I shall buy some rye and barley seed that is all mine, and then I shall sow it in my mother's cornfields at home."

The boy smiled to himself, tiptoeing closer to the sleeping fox, which was still quite unaware of his presence.

"Soon my grain will grow tall and ripe," the boy continued, warming up to the idea. "When grand people pass by my large fields of barley and rye they'll say, 'Oh, what splendid and amazing crops that boy has!'

Then I shall say to them, 'Hey, you people! Keep away from my barley and rye!' But they won't listen to me."

Louder now, the boy continued, "So then I shall shout to them, 'HEY! I said to keep away from my barley and rye!' But still they won't take any notice of me. So then, at the top of my voice, I shall scream, 'I TOLD YOU TO KEEP AWAY FROM MY FIELDS!' Yes, that will make them listen to me!"

The foolish boy screamed so loudly that the fox woke up, startled, and ran off at once into the thick forest. The fox was gone so quickly that the boy did not so much as touch a single hair on its back. All of the boy's fine plans disappeared with the fox. As the saying goes:

Take what you can,
while it lies within reach,
But of deeds undone,
don't ever screech!

THE POOR MAN
AND THE FLASK OF OIL

There was once a poor man who lived an honest and simple life. His house was small but clean and warm, and his roof didn't leak. The man's clothes were of simple cotton but clean and certainly not rags. He had plain but adequate food for his table so, although he sometimes felt hungry, he did not starve. For the most part, the poor man was content with his life.

Next door to his modest house stood a fine mansion, which was the home of a wealthy merchant who had riches of every kind and wanted for nothing.

His fancy clothes were tailored in luxurious fabrics of silk and velvet. He dined extravagantly at a hand-carved wooden table, which groaned under the weight of gold plates piled high with every kind of food imaginable. The walls were decorated with hangings of embroidered silk and tapestries in rich sapphire, ruby, and emerald colors.

The merchant had worked long and hard for his wealth by selling oil and honey. His success had brought him riches beyond his expectations, but his life was rich in other ways, too.

The merchant was a kind and generous man, and it gave him great pleasure to share his good fortune.

One day the merchant sent a flask of oil to his needy neighbor, who was delighted with the gift. He set it down carefully on the top shelf.

There the flask sat for a number of days, the poor man's pride and joy.

One day the poor man stood leaning upon his cane as he gazed in awe at his wealthy neighbor's precious gift. At last the man began thinking to himself, "I wonder how much oil there is in that flask. Without doubt there must be a large quantity."

Before long, one thought led to another, and very soon the man got carried away by his imagination.

"If I should sell that flask of oil, I could buy five sheep," he said to himself. "Every spring my sheep should bring forth lambs. By and by, I should own a great flock of sheep. Then I should sell some of the sheep. Perhaps then I could find a wonderful woman who wants to be my wife."

The poor man smiled to himself, lost in his thoughts as one daydream led to another.

"Perhaps my wife and I might have a child," he continued, "and what a fine child we would have—so smart, strong, and happy!"

He drew a deep breath and smiled. "We will play games, like stickball . . ." he said as he raised the cane that he still held in his hand like a bat. "Our child will be a great athlete!"

With these words, the poor man swung the cane to hit an imaginary ball. As he did so, he knocked the flask off the shelf so that the oil ran over him from head to foot. The man's happy daydreams trickled away along with the oil.

THE THREE WISE SAYINGS

One warm, sunny day an old woman was walking in her garden when she noticed a small bird trapped in a net. As she approached the bird, she got the surprise of her life: it suddenly spoke.

"Good woman, do not lock me in a cage, for I am neither beautiful nor entertaining. I am not even able to sing. So, I beg of you, please set me free and, in return, I will be kind and reward you with three wise sayings."

The old woman looked scornfully at the unattractive little bird.

"Indeed," she said, "you are certainly not beautiful, and you say that you cannot sing or entertain me. But if you are able to teach me anything, then I shall set you free. Speak, bird."

"First," said the bird, "do not grieve over things that have already happened. Second, do not wish for things that you cannot have. And, third, never believe all you are told."

The old woman tilted her head thoughtfully and said, "You have indeed taught me something. For sharing such wisdom I will give you your freedom."

She thought about the three sayings as she released the talking bird. The woman felt pleased with herself—that is, until a cackling sound made her look up.

In the tree above, the bird was sitting and laughing quietly as it watched her.

"What's so funny?" shouted the old woman.

"My easily won freedom," the bird replied, adding, "If you had been as clever as I, then you could have become rich."

"How's that?" asked the old woman.

"Instead of letting me go, you should have kept me," the bird replied, "for in my body I have a diamond the size of a hen's egg."

The old woman, at a loss for words, stared long and hard at the bird, until, at last, she spoke.

"You think freedom will make you happy? It's summer now. The fields and trees are green, but soon it will be winter. All the streams and ponds will freeze over, and you won't find a drop to drink. Snow will cover the land, and you will find nothing to eat. But I can keep you warm and sheltered from the bitter winds of winter."

She continued, "You shall have plenty of food and water without even having to search for them."

But the little bird only laughed louder.

"Foolish woman," it said, "I told you three wise sayings, but you have learned nothing. I earned my freedom fairly, but you forgot my sayings within just a few minutes."

The bird laughed again as it looked down, just out of reach of the angry old woman.

"Do you remember what I said? You should not grieve over things that have already happened, but still you grieve about giving me my freedom. You should not wish for things that you cannot have, and yet you want me, who will never be imprisoned willingly. You should not believe all you are told, yet you believe that inside my body rests a diamond as large as a hen's egg. I am barely half that size myself!"

And with that, the bird flew away.

THE ARCHER AND THE RABBIT

One day an archer caught a little gray and white rabbit in the clearing of a forest. The rabbit was trapped in the archer's nets and could not get free.

"You are very small," the archer said, "but you might still make a tasty snack."

The archer was about to kill the rabbit, not knowing her special gift. Unlike other rabbits, she had the gift of speech. Knowing that her life was at risk, the rabbit wasted no time in addressing the archer.

"What do you gain by killing me?" she pleaded. "I am very small and cannot satisfy your appetite. Let me go, I beg you, and in return I will reward you with three wise sayings. If you follow their advice precisely, you have everything to gain and nothing to lose."

The archer, astonished at hearing the rabbit speak, promised the rabbit her freedom on the conditions she had described.

"Listen, then," the rabbit said, softly.
"First, never attempt the impossible.
Second, do not regret the loss of
something you cannot regain. Third,
do not believe things that are incredible.
If you remember these three sayings,
their wisdom will profit you beyond
all measure."

The man, honoring his promise, let the rabbit escape. Quickly, the rabbit hopped away to the edge of the clearing. The man watched the rabbit go, feeling good about himself for being so generous. At the edge of the clearing the rabbit spoke again to the archer.

"You are a foolish man," she said, "for today you have lost a great treasure. Hidden in my stomach is a perfect pearl. Not only is it flawless in its beauty, but it is bigger than even the egg of an ostrich."

The archer stamped his foot in anger at his loss, loaded his bow, and pointed an arrow straight at the rabbit. But then he imagined the damage that his arrow might cause to the pearl that lay inside the rabbit.

The rabbit laughed mockingly but remained out of reach. The archer threw down his bow and arrow and shook his fist.

"I must trap this rabbit carefully," he told himself, shaking his head in regret at the rabbit's escape.

Immediately the archer had an idea. He spread his nets and tried to trap her a second time. Sometimes she hopped close, to taunt him, but for all his attempts, the rabbit escaped the archer.

"Come into my house, sweet rabbit," he urged, "and I will show you every kindness. I will feed you with my own hand and let you roam around freely, wherever and whenever you wish."

The rabbit answered, "You have just proven yourself to be the fool that I always thought you were." The rabbit stood up on her hind legs.

"You paid no attention to the advice I gave you," the rabbit continued. "Never attempt the impossible, do not regret the loss of something you cannot regain, and do not believe things that are incredible. You cannot catch me again, yet you have spread your nets to do just that."

"Furthermore," the rabbit laughed, "you believe that my stomach contains a precious pearl larger than the egg of an ostrich, when I myself am nowhere near that size! You are a fool and a fool you will always remain!"

With these cold words, the rabbit hopped out of sight. The archer returned sorrowfully to his own house. He never again caught sight of the rabbit.